MANAGING
DISAGREEMENT
CONSTRUCTIVELY

MANAGING DISAGREEMENT CONSTRUCTIVELY

Herbert S Kindler

KOGAN
PAGE

Acknowledgements

Marilyn Ginsburg, MFCC in private practice, helped significantly in the development of the book's conceptual framework, original research and manuscript editing.

Eric L Herzog, PhD, consultant, collaborated in designing the initial workshop and supporting materials presented at the Atlantic Richfield Company.

Robin D Willits, PhD, professor of management at the University of New Hampshire, provided review comments that were helpful in making the book more cohesive and precise.

Charles M Vance, PhD, assistant professor of human resources development at Loyola Marymount University, provided insightful suggestions.

Editor Mike Crisp's diligent editing contributed importantly to the book's readability.

First published in the United States of America
in 1986 by Crisp Publications Inc, 95 First Street,
Los Altos, California 94022, USA. Second Edition 1988.

This edition first published in Great Britain in
1988 by Kogan Page Ltd, 120 Pentonville Road,
London N1 9JN

British Library Cataloguing in Publication Data

Kindler, Herbert S.
  Managing disagreement constructively
  1.Business firms. Management. Techniques
  I. Title
  658.4

  ISBN 1–85091–811–2
  ISBN 1–85091–812–0 Pbk

Typeset by DP Photosetting, Aylesbury, Bucks
Printed and bound in Great Britain by
Dotesios Printers Ltd

Contents

Acknowledgements   4

About This Book   7

Preface   9

Introduction   11

Guiding Principles   12

Overview   14

Phase 1. Diagnosis   16
   1. Clarify critical issues *18*
   2. Identify stakeholders *19*
   3. Assess sources of conflict *20*

Phase 2. Planning   27
   1. Recognise your patterns *27*
   2. Minimise pitfalls *45*
   3. Plan your strategy *51*

Phase 3. Preparation   56
   1. Use a problem-solving framework *56*
   2. Practise *63*
   Observer guide *69*

Phase 4. Implementation   72
  1. Carry out the plan *72*
  2. Evaluate outcomes *79*
  3. Take follow-up action *81*
  Reflection *82*

Summary   83

Further Reading   86

About This Book

Managing Disagreement Constructively stands out from other books in an important way. It's not a book to read – it's a book to *use*. The unique 'self-paced' format of this book and the many worksheets encourage the reader to get involved and try some new ideas immediately.

This book will introduce the critical building blocks of how to manage conflict constructively. Using the simple yet sound techniques presented can make a dramatic change in one's ability to handle potentially destructive conflict in a positive, constructive way. It can be used effectively in a number of ways. Here are some possibilities:

Individual study. Because the book is self-instructional, all that is needed is a quiet place, some time and a pencil. By completing the activities and exercises, a reader should not only receive valuable feedback, but also take practical steps for self-improvement.

Workshops and seminars. The book is ideal for assigned reading prior to a workshop or seminar. With the basics in hand, the quality of the participation will improve and more time can be spent on concept extensions and applications during the programme. The book is also effective when it is distributed at the beginning of a session, and participants work through the contents.

Open learning. Books can be used by those unable to attend 'home office' training sessions.

There are several other possibilities that depend on the objectives, programme or ideas of the user.

Preface

The constructive handling of disagreement is central to personal satisfaction and organisational effectiveness. Improved skills in managing interpersonal differences will enrich your work, relationships and career.

This book helps you to:

- anticipate and prevent destructive conflict;
- deal with disagreement before it erupts out of control;
- encourage the expression of differences when confronting them would be beneficial;
- manage disagreement with more skill and assurance.

The book can be used in a training workshop, and also for self-study. Structured learning exercises help the individual reader to 'learn from doing' as well as from reading. Therefore, as you read through the book, you will be invited to complete clarifying exercises.

No pat prescriptions are offered; rather, possibilities are presented to help you apply these concepts in practical, everyday situations.

Herbert S Kindler, PhD

Introduction

Disagreement among people in relationships, groups and organisations comes with the territory. It's common to hear:

'What I dislike most about disagreement is the endless arguing and having to listen to someone else's stored-up anger and resentment. I can do without it.'

'We could be doing something a lot more productive than dancing around our differences. It's a waste of time because people don't really change their minds anyway.'

'I could be understanding and listen to why a worker doesn't want to follow my instructions, but all I'm going to get for my trouble is that others will start questioning what I say and I'll be seen by my boss as a weak manager. As far as I'm concerned, nice guys finish last.'

Every encounter with someone whose views differ from our own offers the potential for friction, wasted time, bruised feelings and looking foolish.

Managing interpersonal differences isn't easy. Signs of mismanagement are everywhere – back-biting rivalry, bitter divorces, bickering colleagues. Mishandling these differences leaves emotional scars, diverts energy from where it's really needed and undermines morale. No wonder so many people walk away from disagreement. Despite the risk of pain and irritation, however, the rewards for handling disagreement constructively are gratifying.

Guiding Principles

As you review the concepts and techniques for managing disagreement presented in this book, the following philosophy is valuable. Its essence is to honour the legitimate interests of all involved persons.

1. Preserve dignity and self-respect

Preserve and protect the dignity of all *stakeholders* (shorthand for 'people who have an important stake in issues under consideration'), including your own. In a heated discussion, it's easy to say something demeaning. Keep your focus on *issues*, not personalities. Until proved otherwise, assume the other person is expressing a legitimate concern when disagreeing. Even if someone who disagrees with you appears stubborn or stupid, you won't get closer to resolving a dispute by putting them down.

2. Listen with empathy

When you listen to another's views, put yourself in their shoes. See from that person's perspective; feel the speaker's emotional state. When ideas conflict with what you already believe, notice if you discount the speaker's message. If body language or feeling tone communicate an uncaring or hostile attitude, do you respond defensively? To get all the information basic to managing differences, you need to listen with a neutrality that suspends critical judgement. When you listen to understand fully, you convey the message: 'I respect you as a person. Your thoughts and feelings are important to me whether or not I agree with them.'*

3. Don't expect to change others' behavioural style

This book deals with *interdependent relationships*, where each person depends on the other for satisfaction or getting a job done. Because stakes are high, the reflex reaction to disagreement is the desire to change the other person's basic behavioural style. Changing your own behaviour is hard enough; it requires sensitive awareness, compelling motivation and resolute persistence. Changing behavioural traits of another is almost impossible in the course of handling a dispute. Rather, focus on what *you* say and do when you're with a 'difficult' person. Behaviour is automatically transformed when *either* person changes their customary pattern of relating to the other.

4. Express your independent perspective

When you're the lone dissenter, it's tempting to surrender your conviction to conform with more popular views. At other times, it's easy to get so embroiled in a heated dispute that you lose yourself, and the war, to win a battle. Your *gift* to others is your independent point of view – which requires that you understand and reflect about what really matters to *you*. Once your perspective and concerns have been shared, be willing to embrace an alternative view that allows needed action to be taken.

These guidelines – preserving dignity, listening for the message even if you don't agree with it, respecting others as they are and expressing your views – comprise an attitudinal framework helpful in resolving disagreement. With these principles, you communicate: 'I honour you and your needs. I take responsibility for letting you know where I stand. We can manage our differences constructively.'

---

* For an excellent book on listening the publisher recommends *A Practical Guide to Effective Listening* by Diane Bone (Kogan Page).

Overview

As important as a guiding philosophy is, alone it won't ensure the constructive resolution of differences. A systematic process for dealing with disagreement is vital to producing desirable outcomes. This book presents such a step-by-step process.

The approach requires:

1. Anticipating disagreement before it boils over into heated conflict
2. Planning an appropriate strategy
3. Preparing to set your strategy in motion
4. Taking action (or planned inaction) and checking the results.

Figure 1 graphically presents the framework for this approach.

Everyone has lapses when, in a heated moment, something unnecessarily abrasive is said. Most people and most relationships are resilient enough to take occasional rough treatment. However, rather than dissipate energy and goodwill in testy disputes, more constructive paths open when you apply a *systematic process* and *broad repertoire of strategies*.

Each of the four process phases shown in Figure 1, and each of the nine relevant strategies, will be elaborated in the following pages.

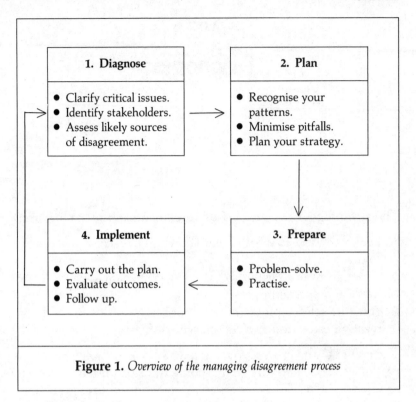

Figure 1. *Overview of the managing disagreement process*

PHASE 1
Diagnosis

The advantages of diagnosing disagreements in the making are:

- You can choose to what extent you want to become personally involved.
- You gain time to listen to others, gather data, develop your views and decide if opposition is likely.
- You can select and refine an appropriate strategy, perhaps averting escalation to a full-blown conflict.

The power of the process covered in this book is that it applies to real-life issues. Therefore, at this point, think of a situation where a view you hold is *likely to be opposed* by someone whose agreement or cooperation you need. The setting can be either at work or in your personal life.

If a disagreement doesn't immediately come to mind, focus on a recent or imminent *change* in your organisational or private life. Sometimes change breeds conflict; sometimes conflict begets change. In either event, the potential for disagreement is rooted in change.

Because we shall be referring back to the situation you develop, write in a description of *a disagreement that is developing (or has developed) that really matters to you*. Include what led up to the present state of affairs and its current status.

Description of your current (or potential) disagreement

_____

_____

_____

_____

_____

_____

_____

_____

_____

_____

_____

_____

_____

A real-life situation that provides another frame of reference follows. Think about how you would have handled this situation if you were Mary's manager.

Case study 1: Petty cash

Mary, a meticulous, hard-working employee, had been with the Ajax Company for seven years before any problem developed with her performance. Mary had started as a secretary and progressively moved up to head bookkeeper. As such, she was responsible for a large, active petty cash fund.

During a spot check, her boss Edwin noticed pencil erasures on expense reports, even though employees had been directed by memo to record their expenses in ink. When Edwin confronted her, Mary confessed to temporarily 'borrowing' £300 from petty cash. She explained that her mother had been in and out of nursing homes for two years and had exhausted the family's resources and credit. Mary said that she used the petty cash to pay her mother's latest bill. Edwin told Mary that he would consult the managing director, Henry, and let her know what was decided.

When he consulted Henry, Edwin said he didn't want to sidestep his responsibility and, though he planned to make the final decision, Edwin wanted the benefit of the MD's thinking. Edwin said that his course of action was clear: any employee who steals should be dismissed. Henry felt uncomfortable applying Edwin's principle to Mary's case, and wasn't sure what to do.

We'll return to your situation and to this case as we move further into the diagnostic phase of managing disagreement. With your narrative, you've already started to diagnose where important disagreement may be brewing. You can sharpen your diagnostic skills by using the following three-step process.

Step 1. Clarify critical issues

To diagnose budding disagreement, you need to learn if your initial views on core issues are shared by other stakeholders.

Your key is *honest feedback*. However, when the people you count on are in a hierarchical role relationship (such as boss-subordinate, teacher-student, parent-child), they may not feel safe expressing disagreement. They may not want to risk saying, 'I feel you're wrong' or even, 'I see this issue differently.' Subordinates, for example, may not want to take a position that might hurt their careers. They don't want to have their views brushed aside, or be seen as odd or uncooperative. Subordinates generally accept as a self-evident truth the maxim, confirmed by social psychologists: you create less trouble for yourself by agreeing with your boss. Therefore, *don't expect critical feedback to be freely volunteered*. To learn views that differ from your own, you can do the following:

- *Model the desired level of openness*, allowing yourself to be appropriately vulnerable. For example, if warranted by the situation, express your own fears, doubts and concerns.

- *Ask for feedback* – and don't punish those who then tell you something you didn't want to hear.
- Explain *why* you want feedback – for example, to stimulate innovation, realise mutual gain, or create a more satisfying relationship.
- Look for *non-verbal cues*, especially from people who may not feel comfortable articulating their disagreement. Notice if verbal and non-verbal messages correspond. For example, is your boss saying, 'Take all the time you need,' while he nervously packs his briefcase and glances at his watch?

To learn where the views of others diverge from your own, *help them to disagree with you.*

Step 2. Identify stakeholders

Think about the potential conflict you've described on pages 16–17. Write the names of those persons who have a vested interest in the outcome of the events in your narrative. Include individuals who have to implement decisions or live with them. Indicate each stakeholder's position or relationship to you. (*Note.* You will usually want to take this step concurrently with Step 1.)

Stakeholder's name   *Position or relationship*

_____   _____

_____   _____

_____   _____

_____   _____

_____   _____

_____   _____

The stakeholders in the 'Petty cash' narrative were:

Mary	Head bookkeeper, reports to Edwin
Edwin	Controller, Mary's boss
Henry	Managing Director, Edwin's boss

Board of directors	Henry's bosses
Stockholders	Owners
Other employees	People most affected by any precedent that might be set by Mary's treatment.

Note. While your list of stakeholders may be limited to your main 'characters', also consider others who are likely to be most concerned with or affected by the resolution of your disagreement.

Step 3. Assess sources of conflict

Seeds of conflict are sown when stakeholders believe that a proposed course of action involves:

1. inaccurate or incomplete information;
2. inappropriate or seemingly incompatible goals;
3. ineffective or unacceptable methods;
4. antagonistic or other negative feelings.

Each of these categories is a potential source of conflict. Your responses to the following questions will help you probe each category and facilitate your diagnosis.

Potential source of conflict 1
Inaccurate or incomplete information
To avoid misunderstanding the *facts*, answer these questions:

- Do stakeholders have full *access to the same information*? For example, are upper-level managers missing critical operating details or the most current data? Have estimates been exaggerated to make someone look good – such as a favoured supplier? Are less informed employees missing part of the big picture (like blind men feeling different parts of an elephant and drawing vastly different conclusions about the nature of the animal)?
- Is the same information being *interpreted differently*? Perceptions are influenced by social conditioning, personal history and vested interests. One person interprets an event as a challenging opportunity, another sees it as a threat. One person sees

savings in a proposal to automate, another sees higher costs. One person sees a report as definitive, another sees it as obscure or ambiguous. As you look at the drawing below, for example, do you see a vase, two faces, or both? Different people can interpret an identical object differently.

Write below, *for your situation*, how you will ensure that the stakeholders have accurate and complete information.

_____

_____

_____

_____

_____

_____

_____

To be sure, Henry had accurate information in the 'Petty cash' case; Edwin was instructed to check with the nursing home to find out if Mary had, in fact, paid them £300 as she claimed. Henry also asked to have earlier expense reports examined for erasures or other signs of alteration to find out if Mary's offence was a one-time aberration.

Potential source of conflict 2
Inappropriate or seemingly incompatible goals

When the goals of interdependent people diverge or clash, hopeless disagreement is *not* inevitable. Disagreement over goals usually occurs at *one level* of concern. However, a higher level can almost always be found where stakeholders share a common vision or goal. Identify this *common ground*. It's a solid starting point where agreement already exists.

For example, labour and management may disagree over wages, but if both parties agree that a primary goal is for the organisation to remain viable, a foundation to build on is in place.

Write below, *for your situation*, superordinate goals that are consonant with stakeholder needs and wants.

_____

_____

_____

_____

_____

_____

_____

_____

_____

In the 'Petty cash' case, Edwin's and Henry's goals appear to clash.

Edwin believes it is the responsibility of a chartered accountant to dismiss anyone who is dishonest. Henry questions whether dismissal is fair if compelling or extenuating circumstances exist. However, at another level, Edwin and Henry do agree on two superordinate goals. They want employees who can be trusted in situations where their honesty isn't tested by avoidable temptation or enticement; and they want an effective and efficient system for handling petty cash.

Potential source of conflict 3
Ineffective or unacceptable methods

Disagreement may exist over methods for completing a task – the techniques and procedures that different people prefer. The following diagnostic checklist can help you to identify and examine disagreement associated with methods.

- [ ] Does good *alignment* exist between a task to be accomplished and the person asked to perform it? That is, are the skills and interests of individuals well matched to the jobs they are asked to perform?
- [ ] Is the required task *well formulated*? Specifically, have clear and reasonable boundaries been set? Are the responsibilities coordinated so that activities mesh effectively? Has adequate authority been delegated?
- [ ] Is enough *support* being provided? Do people have adequate resources, facilities, training and recognition? Do they have appropriate input into decisions that affect their efforts?
- [ ] Are acceptable *ethical standards* being followed? Do employees use their organisational position for personal benefit? Are moral standards espoused but not practised? For example, if a father always preaches 'obey the law' to his children, does he also buy a radar detector for his car so he won't get caught speeding?

Disagreement over methods entails three factors:

1. How people *weigh the odds* that one procedure will be more effective than another in reaching a common goal.
2. How people *assess personal costs*. For example, a method accept-

able to one person may be so time-consuming that another person can't pursue other high priority goals.

3. *Personal values and ethical concerns.*

For your situation, write below the issues you want to examine more deeply regarding methods and values.

_____

_____

_____

_____

_____

_____

_____

_____

In the 'Petty cash' case, Henry decided to explore the way Mary went about meeting her need for cash. Why didn't she consult Edwin during the two-year period her mother was seriously ill? Had Edwin and Henry been too aloof from their employees? Why weren't employees following the written instructions about completing their expense reports in ink? How could the company's method of handling cash be improved for better efficiency and less temptation? Should a written policy for making loans to employees be developed? Is an employee assistance programme needed? Should the company medical insurance have optional coverage for employees' parents? Is Ajax Company morally responsible to make the issues public by charging embezzlement in a court of law?

Potential source of conflict 4
Antagonistic or other negative feelings
Disagreement, when it surfaces, may have a long history. Left-over resentment from previously mismanaged conflicts tends to

linger. People who have been demeaned or feel betrayed may act in punishing ways to even the score. When disagreement stems from old wounds, it may be difficult to diagnose because it is rarely acknowledged and often masquerades as a 'personality clash'.

Not all negative feelings come from interpersonal conflict. Other sources include discouragement with general inefficiency, or frustration from intergroup rivalry.

As you diagnose *your situation*, write how long the disagreement you described may have been incubating, and if those involved appear to be rivals.

_____

_____

_____

_____

_____

_____

_____

_____

_____

_____

_____

In the 'Petty cash' case, when Mary moved into positions of greater responsibility, perhaps she didn't feel adequately compensated. If her communication with her boss was poor, and the facts suggest this possibility, Mary's stealing may have been influenced by feelings of resentment and the rationale: 'It's money I should have been getting all along, anyway.'

Note. In the diagnostic phase, you are attempting to ferret out all *potential causes* of disagreement. You may raise more questions than you need to resolve immediately. For example, to handle Mary's petty cash, it was not necessary to extend insurance coverage. However, the sooner diagnostic questions are addressed, the sooner you will be in a position to avert needless future conflict.

PHASE 2
Planning

Your diagnosis framed the central issues, identified stakeholders and suggested likely sources of disagreement. At this point, you are ready to plan a strategy for dealing with relevant differing views.

Step 1. Recognise your patterns

Most people bring relatively *stable patterns of behaviour*, or styles, to the resolution of disputes. The common element in all your disagreements is *you*. Therefore, start by gathering information about your own typical behaviour. Although it's difficult to see yourself as others see you, the following exercises will help you to recognise patterns you've developed for dealing with conflict.

To benefit fully, complete each exercise as though you are personally involved and have a real stake in the outcome.

Exercise 1: Allocating fixed resources

Assume you are one of three people who will be given £500 if you are willing to play a game and abide by its rules. The fourth person in the game is a timekeeper. The rules are: You and the two other players are to meet and each will receive £500. At this meeting, with no preliminary discussion, you have a maximum of seven minutes to reallocate the group's £1,500. However, one of you is to leave the meeting with *no* money. The other two players may divide the £1,500 in any fashion. No hidden deals are allowed – that is, you can't arrange to pay off one person if he or she drops a claim to a share of the money during the game. The timekeeper will announce the time remaining at one-minute intervals. If seven minutes elapse and the reallocation hasn't been completed in accordance with the rules, then the timekeeper gets the entire £1,500.

Imagine yourself as one of the three players. (Better still, you may want to try the game with friends, using monopoly money or smaller real sums. For example, each player might contribute £20 and, for realism, at least one person doesn't get it back.) Write below the approach or *strategy you plan to use.*

_____

_____

_____

_____

_____

_____

_____

Two initial strategies are most common. Interestingly, the most popular one almost always fails and sooner or later is abandoned. It's a *selling* approach. That is, one player tries to convince the other two that his or her needs are the most worthy or the most desperate. When persuasion fails, as it usually does – because it's hard to convince anyone to walk away from £500 – the players often switch to a second strategy. They agree on a *decision rule* that appears fair. The usual rule is some form of lottery, like a short straw or odd coin out. On rare occasions, *force* is used – that is, one person grabs the money and holds it for seven minutes. Finally, some players *collaborate*, asking: 'Can we turn this win-lose game into a win-win situation?'* They sometimes discover a charity to

_____

* A win-win situation is one in which the two participants each feel they have gained. A win-lose situation is one in which one participant feels he or she has gained nothing and that the other has gained everything.

which they can all agree to make a donation. Then they typically give everything to a player who appears trustworthy for contribution to the charity.

The object of this exercise, and those that follow, is not to get the 'right' answer, but to look for patterns.

What was your preferred strategy? Did you select a *selling* approach to convince the other players that your needs were most compelling? Did you propose a *decision rule* to stop the clock? Did you settle your differences by domination, using force or threats? Did you consider a *collaborative* strategy to reach a superordinate goal?

The following exercise applies to an organisational setting. Again, it enables you to collect additional information about your preferred styles for managing disagreement.

Exercise 2: Personal business at work

This case concerns a subordinate doing personal work in the office. Assume you are this employee's boss. After reading the case, *rank* the five options, A to E, in the spaces provided. Use '1' to indicate the *most* appropriate option, '5' for the *least* appropriate option.

As supervisor of a 12-person design section, you notice that one of your designers is drafting plans for an addition to her house. She is an employee whose competence and initiative you value. When you ask why she's working on a personal project during company hours, she says that she has caught up on all high priority work and lacks adequate drafting equipment at home. You also know she has done some non-drafting work on rush projects for the company on her own time at home.

Rank your options below.

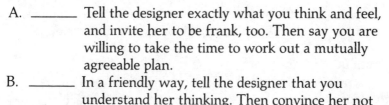

A. _____ Tell the designer exactly what you think and feel, and invite her to be frank, too. Then say you are willing to take the time to work out a mutually agreeable plan.

B. _____ In a friendly way, tell the designer that you understand her thinking. Then convince her not to work on personal projects in the office because it sets a precedent for other employees who may not be as willing as she is to do work at home.

C. _____ Ignore the situation. Deal with future problems, if any, when they come up.

D. _____ Offer to let the designer continue to use the equipment for personal projects, but only after 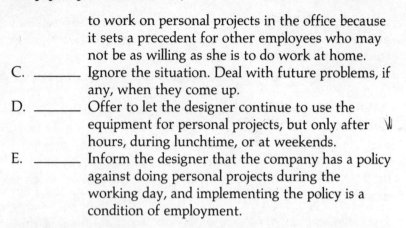 hours, during lunchtime, or at weekends.

E. _____ Inform the designer that the company has a policy against doing personal projects during the working day, and implementing the policy is a condition of employment.

You can extend this exercise by asking one or more friends or colleagues to provide their rankings independent of one another. Then see, as a group, if you can arrive at a single group ranking. If the deliberations drag on, set a time limit. Notice what processes *you* use in attempting to gain group agreement.

During group discussions, based on this option-ranking exercise, participants expressed the views indicated on the following pages. Their comments illustrate the widely diverse views that capable people can generate.

Option A
Tell the designer exactly what you think and feel, and invite her to be frank, too. Then say you are willing to take the time to work out a mutually agreeable plan.

Comments
For: In this *collaborative* strategy, the subordinate feels respected by her boss because her views are taken into account as they work out a mutually agreeable plan.

Against: This is a weak management style in which the boss fails to take responsibility for what must be done.

Option B
In a friendly way, tell the designer that you understand her thinking. Then convince her not to work on personal projects in

the office because it sets a precedent for other employees who may not be as willing as she is to do work at home.

Comments

For: This option enables the boss to *smooth over* differences without wasting time in long, fruitless debate.

Against: The boss doesn't get the benefit of the employee's views, and may discourage her future initiative.

Option C
Ignore the situation. Deal with future problems, if any, when they come up.

Comments

For: When 12 people work together for any length of time, everyone knows the diligent employees who take work home. There's no danger of setting a troublesome precedent. As the saying goes, 'If something isn't broken, don't fix it.'

Against: This *maintenance* strategy, by inaction, tacitly accepts the subordinate's behaviour and creates an undesirable precedent that may escalate in the future.

Option D
Offer to let the designer continue to use the equipment for personal projects, but only after hours, during lunchtime, or at weekends.

Comments

For: In this *bargaining* strategy, the boss gains goodwill with the employee by allowing her to satisfy a personal need at minimal cost to the organisation.

Against: The boss may unknowingly be subjecting the company to potential liability. For example, if the employee hurts herself while at work during a weekend without supervision, the company may be liable.

Option E

Inform the designer that the company has a policy against doing personal projects during the working day, and implementing the policy is a condition of employment.

Comments

For: Following a specific company *rule* definitively settles the issue. In this situation, because the policy is a *condition of employment* (which means that deviation from the policy requires automatic dismissal), a manager can't afford to ignore it.

Against: For the boss simply to recite a company policy leaves the employee feeling her boss doesn't really care about her competence, loyalty or initiative.

Exercises 1 and 2 were designed to get you thinking about how to deal with others who hold views different from your own. Exercise 3 consists of completing the *Management of Differences Inventory* (MODI-self). It provides a *systematic overview* which heightens self-awareness about how you manage disagreement at present.

Exercise 3: Management of differences inventory, MODI-self©

On the following pages are pairs of statements that describe alternative ways to respond to situations involving differing views.

When you deal with differences with others, you may respond one way at one time and another way at another, depending on the situation and who is involved. The inventory takes this into account by providing you with three points to distribute between two statements to show how frequently you relate to others in each of the two ways indicated.

If you respond very differently with different people, you may complete a MODI-self inventory for each person with whom you frequently interact.

Focus on how you actually behave rather than on how you might like to behave, or how you might like others to think you behave. There are no right or wrong answers.

For each pair of statements that follow, allocate *exactly three points* between the alternatives to show how frequently you behave as described:

3 = very often, 2 = moderately often,
1 = occasionally, 0 = rarely or never

Use only whole numbers, not fractions.

Example
In a disagreement, dispute or difference of view with another:

---

0 (a) ☐ I set out to win the argument.   (a) 2   (a) 1   (a) 0
                                   OR   **OR**   **OR**

   (b) ☐ I withdraw to check my facts.   (b) 1   (b) 2   (b) 3

Note that each *pair of scores* must add up to 3.

Nine strategic styles and their use

Just as serious golfers play best with a full set of clubs, you can more effectively handle the sand traps of disagreement with a wide range of strategic styles.

The MODI provided you with scores for nine strategic styles. You can take any of these from your 'bag' whenever you manage interpersonal differences. Before you can interpret the specific scores for each style, however, you need to understand how it works, and where it works. Let's begin with background information.

When MODI was developed, executives were interviewed who were regarded by their colleagues as skilful in managing disagreement. They were asked: 'When your views on a work-related issue differ from the views of others who also are importantly involved, how do you prepare to handle such situations?'

In a disagreement, dispute or difference of view with another:

1(a) ☐ I let emotions cool before taking decisive action.
  (b) ☐ I find some formula or criterion we both agree on.

2(a) ☐ I assert myself to gain what I am after.
  (b) ☐ We jointly develop a mutually agreeable plan that merges both views.

3(a) ☐ I continue to follow my view and the other person continues to follow his or her view.
  (b) ☐ I yield on some points to get my way on others.

4(a) ☐ I place more emphasis on similarities and less on differences.
  (b) ☐ I find logical rules we both agree on as the basis for our decision.

5(a) ☐ We take action that lets both parties retain their initial positions, at least on an interim basis.
  (b) ☐ Within agreed limits, I give control to the other person while providing encouragement and support.

6(a) ☐ I gain agreement for my position by avoiding details on which we may disagree.
  (b) ☐ I try solutions proposed by the other person.

7(a) ☐ I push to have my approach or my ideas prevail.
  (b) ☐ I accept the views of the other person.

8(a) ☐ We work out a fair combination of losses and gains for both of us.
  (b) ☐ I get both our concerns out in the open, and we problem-solve together.

9(a) ☐ I wait until I feel better prepared to take action.
  (b) ☐ After stating my expectations, I encourage the other person to come up with the answer.

10(a) ☐ I avoid highly emotional scenes that may detract from the point I am making.
  (b) ☐ We agree to disagree, at least for a while or on an experimental basis.

11(a) ☐ I ask a person who disagrees with me to accept my view by emphasising its positive features.
  (b) ☐ I fully express my ideas and feelings, and urge the other person to do the same.

12(a) ☐ We find a formula to resolve our differences.
  (b) ☐ I find solutions in which gains balance losses for both parties.

In a disagreement, dispute or difference of view with another:

13(a) ☐ I get my ideas accepted.
   (b) ☐ I express confidence in the other person by allowing him or her, within limits, to resolve our issue.

14(a) ☐ We mutually agree on rules or procedures to resolve our differences.
   (b) ☐ I accommodate myself to the other person's view.

15(a) ☐ I convince the other person of the merit of my position.
   (b) ☐ We acknowledge and allow each other's differences to exist until appropriate means for resolution become clear.

16(a) ☐ I accept the views expressed by the other person.
   (b) ☐ We openly integrate ideas of both persons.

17(a) ☐ I avoid presenting information likely to hurt the other person's feelings.
   (b) ☐ Within a given framework, I let the other person work out our issue while indicating confidence in him or her.

18(a) ☐ I wait until the other person initiates the first action steps.
   (b) ☐ We find mutually acceptable middle ground on which to resolve our differences.

19(a) ☐ I delay suggesting changes until I feel sure my views will be accepted.
   (b) ☐ I don't resist the views of the other person.

20(a) ☐ We find mutually agreeable objective procedures (such as taking a vote, a lottery or an appropriate test).
   (b) ☐ We find ways to jointly reframe our differences to satisfy both our needs.

21(a) ☐ I give in on some points if the other person is likely to reciprocate.
   (b) ☐ I state my expectations and concerns and let the other person work out our concerns with my encouragement.

22(a) ☐ I show the other person that in the final analysis our views really aren't very different.
   (b) ☐ I give the other person a turn or concession if I believe he or she will do the same for me.

23(a) ☐ I find ways that allow each of us to pursue our individual viewpoints.
   (b) ☐ We find solutions that take both our views fully into account.

24(a) ☐ I deal with differences only after waiting until I feel the time is right.
   (b) ☐ I act in ways that advance my position.

In a disagreement, dispute or difference of view with another:

25(a) ☐ We let a mutually agreeable rule or procedure decide the issue.
  (b) ☐ We find ways in which we can both pursue our respective points of view.

26(a) ☐ I find ways to accept the other person's views.
  (b) ☐ Given acceptable boundaries, I am willing for the other person to deal with our differences while I provide support.

27(a) ☐ I persuade the other person of the merit of my position.
  (b) ☐ I establish an objective basis with the other person for resolving our differences.

28(a) ☐ I put off dealing with our differences until I have enough information to support my position.
  (b) ☐ I resolve our differences by emphasising where we are not so far apart in our thinking.

29(a) ☐ We settle our differences by working out a compromise solution.
  (b) ☐ I agree to follow the other person's approach.

30(a) ☐ I point out that our differences aren't substantial enough to fight over.
  (b) ☐ I oppose the other person's view.

31(a) ☐ We find new perspectives that satisfy both our needs.
  (b) ☐ I defer making changes until I have adequate support to win my position.

32(a) ☐ I don't express all the negative possibilities.
  (b) ☐ I get agreement from the other person to live with our differences, at least for a time.

33(a) ☐ We jointly agree to accept an objective criterion or the decision of a third party as the basis for resolving our differences.
  (b) ☐ Within stated bounds, I encourage and support the other person to take the initiative in dealing with our differences.

34(a) ☐ I play to win.
  (b) ☐ I make adjustments only when the other person is willing to do the same.

35(a) ☐ I urge the other person to take the initiative and, within defined limits, I support his or her decision.
  (b) ☐ We integrate the ideas expressed by both individuals.

36(a) ☐ We agree to follow our separate paths until joint action seems feasible.
  (b) ☐ I accept the other person's ideas.

During these interviews, two concerns emerged as themes: 'How flexible do I want to be as I assert my viewpoint?' and 'How intense do I want my interaction to be with others holding divergent views?'*

The dimension, *viewpoint flexibility*, is concerned with how important and how attainable one's *initial position* appears, and what might be learned by remaining open to other views. The dimension, *interaction intensity*, is concerned with the level of personal involvement and how close or casual a relationship one wants. After the two dimensions – viewpoint flexibility and interaction intensity – emerged, a survey of the literature of management, political science, social psychology, negotiation and organisational behaviour revealed nine strategic styles that formed the model shown in Figure 2, page 41.

These nine strategic styles, alone and in blends, are the tools available to manage disagreement. The labels used to identify each style are intended to be non-judgemental – assuming *all* can be used effectively when well-executed and well-matched to the situation. Keep Figure 2 readily accessible because it will serve you as a powerful ally in dealing with differences.

Following is a description of each strategic style, general application guidelines and an example. In each space provided, cite one specific example that you personally have encountered.

Style 1 ● Maintenance: firm, impersonal
A unilateral decision to maintain the status quo by avoiding or deferring action on differing views. Such non-engagement is usually constructive only as an *interim* strategy.

● *Common sayings.* 'Let well alone.' 'Don't rock the boat.'
● *Application.* When you need time to collect information, enlist support, augment resources or deal with higher priority issues. Also, gains time to build rapport, let emotions cool or allow recent changes to stabilise.

---

* This research is described in 'The Art of Managing Differences', by Herbert S Kindler, *Training & Development Journal*, January 1983.

Strategic style scoring

For each item on pages 34–37, enter your score in the spaces below to determine which strategic styles are used most and least.

1 MAINTENANCE	2 SMOOTHING	3 DOMINATION	4 DECISION RULE	5 COEXISTENCE	6 BARGAINING	7 NON-RESISTANCE	8 SUPPORTIVE RELEASE	9 COLLABORATION
1a =			1b =					
		2a =						2b =
				3a =	3b =			
	4a =		4b =					
				5a =			5b =	
	6a =					6b =		
		7a =				7b =		
					8a =			8b =
9a =							9b =	
10a =				10b =				
	11a =							11b =
			12a =		12b =			
		13a =					13b =	
			14a =			14b =		
		15a =		15b =				
						16a =		16b =

38

TOTAL	1	2	3	4	5	6	7	8	9
	18a =	17a =	24b =	20a =	23a =	18b =	19b =	17b =	20b =
	19a =	22a =	27a =	25a =	25b =	21a =	26a =	21b =	23b =
	24a =	28b =	30b =	27b =	32b =	22b =	29b =	26b =	31b =
	28a =	30a =	34a =	33a =	36a =	29a =	36b =	33b =	35b =
	31a =	32a =				34b =		35a =	
TOTAL	1	2	3	4	5	6	7	8	9

Add the numbers in each column and insert totals above. The sum of the totals *must equal 108*.

- *Example.* 'Joe, the most senior employee in the company, is again generating needless paperwork. However, because he is due to retire in two months, I'll use *maintenance* and defer suggesting changes to improve Joe's system until his successor arrives.'
- *Your example.* _____

_____

_____

_____

_____

Style 2 • Smoothing: firm, moderately personal
Selling your views by accentuating benefits and glossing over, omitting or playing down alternative possibilities.

- *Common sayings.* 'Accentuate the positive.' 'Grease the skids.' 'What he doesn't know won't hurt him.'
- *Application.* When you are clear about your viewpoint, but lack authority to require compliance, or don't have time or energy for a full-scale discussion. Also useful when you want to withhold complete information because you feel it would be hurtful to others, or because they lack the maturity to handle it.
- *Example.* 'Sorry, I can't attend your meeting. It conflicts with my wife's birthday and I'm planning to spend a night in town with her. In choosing between your meeting and the dinner, I know you would want me to come down on the side of *romance*.'
- *Your example.* _____

_____

_____

_____

_____

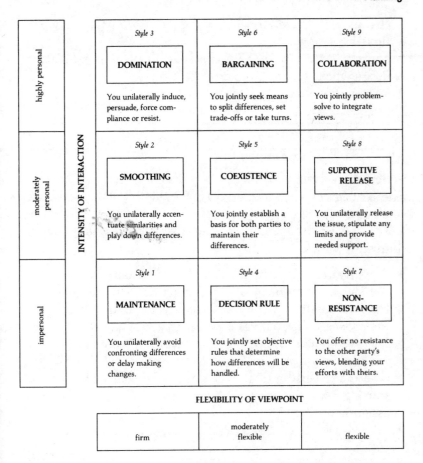

Figure 2. *Nine strategic styles for managing differences between two people or groups with a shared problem*

Style 3 ● Domination: firm, personal
The unilateral use of power and influence to gain compliance with your views.

- *Common sayings.* 'Father knows best.' 'Do it!'
- *Application.* When speed or confidentiality are important; when you believe that others involved have little to offer that would

change your mind; or when the issue is too trivial to waste time discussing.

- *Example.* 'Until you've been checked out on this equipment, here's what I want you to do ...'
- *Your example.* _____

_____

_____

Style 4 ● Decision rule: moderately firm, impersonal
The joint agreement to use an objective rule or external criterion (such as a coin flip, lottery, seniority system, voting procedure, test score or arbitration) as the basis for deciding among competing views.

- *Common sayings.* 'Play by the rules.' 'Let's be fair.'
- *Application.* When being fair and impartial is more important than the specific outcome of a disagreement; or when any of the proposed alternatives is better than a stalemate.
- *Example.* 'Of all those who want to work overtime next week, we need only two. Can we agree on a lottery for those of you who haven't had a turn during the past year, or how about starting a seniority system for offering overtime assignments?'
- *Your example.* _____

_____

_____

Style 5 ● Coexistence: moderately firm, moderately personal
The joint determination to follow separate paths without animosity. Use as an *interim* strategy when it's expensive or confusing to operate two different parallel systems to accomplish the same purpose.

- *Common sayings.* 'Let's agree to disagree.' 'You take the high road, and I'll take the low road.'
- *Application.* When both parties believe they are right, more compelling evidence is needed to persuade one to change

views, and a wrong decision could be irreversible or costly.

- *Example.* 'Let's agree to use both the current manual method and the new automated method for three months until we can see which is most cost-effective.'
- *Your example.* _____

_____

_____

Style 6 ● **Bargaining:** moderately firm, personal
Jointly seeking to exchange something one party wants for something the other party wants through offers and counter-offers.

- *Common sayings.* 'Half a loaf is better than no bread.' 'You scratch my back; I'll scratch yours.'
- *Application.* Use when each party can gain more from an exchange agreement than the best alternative available if no agreement is reached.
- *Example.* 'When we relocate to the new building, if I can have an office with a view, I'm willing to reduce my space to make more room for a conference area.'
- *Your example.* _____

_____

_____

Style 7 ● **Non-resistance:** flexible, impersonal
Even though you disagree with the other person's views, you unilaterally decide to offer no resistance, and to support diligent implementation of required action.

- *Common sayings.* 'Bend with the breeze.' 'Don't win the battle and lose the war.'
- *Application.* Use when you believe the other person has greater expertise than you; or when the issue is of minor importance to you but serious to the other person and you want to be seen as a team player.
- *Example.* 'I've disagreed with my boss's last three ideas, and I

don't like her latest proposal but it's really a minor point in an issue that isn't critical.'

- *Your example.* _____

_____

_____

Style 8 • **Supportive release:** flexible, moderately personal
Even though you disagree with the other person's views, you unilaterally decide to support and encourage that person's initiative within stipulated limits or conditions.

- *Common sayings.* 'Time to try your wings and fly.' 'I support your right to be wrong.'
- *Application.* Use when the other person is capable but lacks confidence, and you want to foster initiative and commitment.
- *Example.* 'Personally, I wouldn't tip off the competition by market-testing the product improvement in Bracknell. But you've studied all the factors more closely than me and, as long as you stay within the budget, I'll go along with your judgement. Let's talk about your results in two weeks.'
- *Your example.* _____

_____

_____

Style 9 • **Collaboration:** flexible, personal
A joint exploration by participants aimed at developing a synthesis of all informed, relevant views. The integration of views is realised through frank discussion of interests, probing of assumptions and by empathetic listening.

- *Common sayings.* 'Let us reason together.' 'Two heads are better than one.'
- *Application.* Use when the issues are too pivotal to be compromised; participants are trustworthy, capable, communicate skilfully and have adequate time for discussion. Use also when participants want to develop a closer relationship, or when commitment of all parties to the selected course of action is

important for a successful outcome.

- *Example.* 'Our product has been implicated in two serious customer accidents. How are we to interpret these events? What action is appropriate for our company to take, and how shall we respond to questions that are being raised by the press?'
- *Your example.* _____

_____

_____

_____

_____

Step 2. Minimise pitfalls

'Red Shoes' is the story of a woman who, when she puts on red ballet shoes, dances like a magnificent prima ballerina, but is unable to stop dancing. This warns that any style we master can be both a blessing and a potential trap.

When we become proficient at anything, we tend to over-use our skill. In childhood, when something works really well, we repeat it. Throughout life, people over-use superior skills – even in situations where they are inappropriate; and neglect developing fledgling skills – even where they would be most useful. When, irrespective of the outcome, one persists in stable, predictable behaviour, others see this preferred pattern as a *personal style*.

In contrast, the term *strategic style* will be reserved for the behaviour that you *consciously choose* to produce a desired outcome.

Neglecting or over-using styles

Your scores on MODI-self (page 33) reflect styles of managing disagreement that you may over- or under-use. Write your scores in the indicated spaces and compare them with the indicated mean scores of 225 middle managers from industry, government and non-profit organisations. If any of your scores are three or more points below the mean, you probably are under-using the style. If your score is three or more points above, you probably are over-using this style. (For the statistically minded reader, three points represents over one standard deviation from the mean scores of the 225 middle managers.)

For any scores three points higher (suggesting *over-use*) or lower (suggesting *neglect*) than the mean, you'll find the following questions helpful for improving your strategic approach. Not all the questions will apply, but those that hit the mark will lead you to broaden your repertoire and make you more effective. For easy comparison, write your scores in the spaces below.

Style 1 ● Maintenance
Manager mean score = 10.2   Your score = _____

If neglected: Do you take the time to collect enough background information? Do you let emotions cool before taking action?

If over-used: Do you wait so long to act that you're seen as unwilling to take reasonable risks? While you gather data, do problems tend to escalate?

Style 2 ● Smoothing
Manager mean score = 11.6   Your score = _____

If neglected: Are you often unable to persuade others, or persuade them of your ideas?

If over-used: Do you appear to others as manipulative or deceptive because they expect you to provide information only if it advances your views?

Style 3 ● Domination
Manager mean score = 10.7   Your score = _____

If neglected: Are you seen as a person who doesn't take a firm stand or have deep convictions? Do you command enough control when you need it?

If over-used: Are you seen as pushy or uncaring about the ideas of others? Have others become too dependent on you? Have you stifled the initiative of others?

Style 4 • Decision rule
Manager mean score = 12.3   Your score = _____

If neglected: Do you waste time discussing differences that aren't important?
If over-used: Do you appear aloof and unwilling to take the heat of personal confrontation, by relying too heavily on impersonal methods to resolve disagreements?

Style 5 • Coexistence
Manager mean score = 11.9   Your score = _____

If neglected: Are you willing to tolerate ambiguity and able to keep several balls in the air? Are you willing to risk being proved wrong by the results of parallel experiments?
If over-used: Do you waste time and resources by allowing too many experiments to coexist?

Style 6 • Bargaining
Manager mean score = 13.7   Your score = _____

If neglected: Are others taking advantage of your tendency not to drive hard enough to win the best deal?
If over-used: Do others start discussions with you by inflating their needs because they anticipate that you will press for concessions?

Style 7 • Non-resistance
Manager mean score = 10.6   Your score = _____

If neglected: Are you seen as uncooperative or not a team player? Do you disagree so often that your views are discounted?
If over-used: Are you seen as an 'apple polisher', more concerned with ingratiating than advocating what you truly believe?

Style 8 • Supportive release
Manager mean score = 12.2   Your score = _____

If neglected: Do you let others learn from their own experience? Do you influence others to develop their initiative?

If over-used: To help others mature, have you taken excessive risks? Have you abdicated your own responsibilities?

Style 9 • Collaboration
Manager mean score = 14.8   Your score = _____

If neglected: Are others demotivated by your failure to invite their participation in decisions that affect them? Are you missing alternative perspectives?

If over-used: Do you avoid taking personal responsibility by using a 'committee' approach? Do you waste too much time holding meetings?

The critical questions just presented are difficult for most people to consider. Everyone has limitations. The goal is to use your scores to become aware of central tendencies so that you can modify well-worn patterns to fit the needs of each situation.

Identify your blocks
Four blocks in particular interfere with the constructive resolution of differences. These blocks are extremes of the two managing-differences dimensions discussed earlier: viewpoint flexibility (the extremes are *rigidity* and *irresolution*); and interaction intensity (extremes are *intrusiveness* and *aloofness*). The following exercise helps you to see where you may be tripping over these blocks.

Exercise 4: Four potential blocks
Tick those items that *generally* apply to your handling of situations where disagreement is involved.

Block I: Rigid behaviour

_____ I get so committed to my views that I have trouble knowing when to give in.

_____ Once I've stated my views openly, I don't like to say I've changed my mind.

_____ I don't take enough time to draw out the opinions of others.

_____ It's difficult to admit when I'm wrong.

Block II: Irresolute behaviour

_____ At meetings, I don't interrupt if others are monopolising the discussion.

_____ I'm willing to forgo my position to keep a harmonious relationship.

_____ Others often push past my views without giving them the consideration they deserve.

_____ I'd rather be a team player than be the only one opposing consensus.

Block III: Intrusive behaviour

_____ I tend to take charge, even when it's not my responsibility.

_____ I protect my interests by maintaining a personal involvement.

_____ The best way to get things done the way I want is to do them myself.

_____ I like to be personally involved, even if it's not necessary to the task at hand.

Block IV: Aloof behaviour

_____ I avoid confrontations that are likely to be emotionally charged.

_____ I avoid getting personally involved if I can delegate responsibility.

_____ Even when others share their feelings, I remain calm and keep my feelings to myself.

_____ I prefer logic to personal persuasion.

> Where you have ticked two or more items for any block, you may have picked up a dysfunctional personal style along the way. Blocks are usually rooted in childhood experiences and social conditioning. For example, you may have been taught by your parents to sidestep differences by saying what is tactful rather than what is truthful. Or, you may have heard, 'If you can't say something nice, don't say anything at all.' However, to command a full range of interpersonal strategies, you must detect and re-examine those deeply etched messages from your past.

Your plan for minimising blocks

Rank from 1 to 4 the blocks presented below in terms of how significant each has been to you in managing disagreement. Use 1 to mean most important and 4 to indicate least important.

Rank   Block

_____   1. *Rigid*
I tend to hold my views too tenaciously, or neglect encouraging others to express alternative views.

_____   2. *Irresolute*
I tend to yield my position too quickly, before others fully appreciate its merits.

_____   3. *Intrusive*
I personally involve myself in disagreements beyond the point of being helpful, or I waste too much time.

_____   4. *Aloof*
I tend to remain too distant, and may give the impression of being uncaring or unconcerned.

To minimise or overcome a potential block to managing disagreement constructively, with respect to the block that I ranked 1 above, I intend to take the following action.

(For example, assume your number one block is *rigid*. You realise that your style at meetings is to run such a tight ship that you tolerate no deviations from the planned agenda. The action you might try is to allow some time at the end of your agenda for others to bring up any item they regard as pressing.)

_____

_____

_____

_____

_____

_____

_____

Step 3. Plan your strategy

You now have access to a wide range of strategies. You have also been asked to appreciate how old habit patterns might block your choosing one (or more) that are appropriate to a given situation. Your next step involves applying this knowledge to select a _strategic style or blend_.

Regarding the specific situation on which you want to focus, you need to decide how firm or flexible to be in your initial position, and how personal or impersonal to be in relation to other stakeholders.

How firm or flexible?

To help you decide how adaptable to be in dealing with other stakeholders on a specific issue, assess the probability that your views will:

1. Advance common goals
2. Be acceptable to other stakeholders
3. Provide a basis for timely action
4. Yield greater benefits and fewer drawbacks than alternative possibilities.

With regard to the situation you described on pages 16–17, to decide how flexibly to hold your views, assess each criterion presented below with a tick. You may want to add brief comments to recall your reasoning later.

1. My views:

Clearly advance common goals	Probably advance common goals	May not advance common goals
☐	☐	☐

Comments: _____

_____

2. My views:

Clearly are acceptable to all stakeholders	Probably are acceptable to all stakeholders	May not be acceptable to all stakeholders
☐	☐	☐

Comments: _____

_____

3. My views:

Clearly permit timely action	Probably permit timely action	May not permit timely action
☐	☐	☐

Comments: _____

_____

4. My views:

Clearly are cost-effective	Probably are cost-effective	May not be cost-effective
☐	☐	☐

Comments: _____

_____

> If *all* ticks are in the first column, this indicates that you feel
> confident you have little to learn or gain in this situation. You
> should consider a *firm* stand. If you have *any* ticks in the third
> column, indicating you are uncertain about at least one important
> criterion, you should consider a *flexible* position. For all other tick
> configurations, a *moderate* stance is likely to be appropriate.
>
> Your viewpoint flexibility: ☐ Firm ☐ Moderate ☐ Flexible

How personal or impersonal?
To help you decide how close a relationship to have while
engaging another stakeholder, consider the following criteria:

1. Are you likely to have a one-off or a continuing relationship?
2. How much satisfaction would you expect from personal
   involvement with this individual?
3. Is this person open to being influenced by face-to-face
   communication?
4. Are you likely to learn more about yourself or develop
   interpersonal skills through engaging this individual?

For your situation on pages 16–17, to decide how personally to
interact, assess each of the following criteria with a tick. Again,
space is provided for brief comments.

1. This relationship will:

Probably continue over time	Possibly continue over time	Probably be a one-off or limited event
☐	☐	☐

Comments: _____

_____

2. Interacting with this person will:

Probably be satisfying	Possibly be satisfying	Probably not be satisfying
☐	☐	☐

Comments: _____

_____

3. This person will:

Probably be open-minded	Possibly be open-minded	Probably not be open-minded
☐	☐	☐

Comments: _____

_____

4. This is a person from whom I will:

Probably learn more about myself or sharpen my skills	Possibly learn more about myself or sharpen my skills	Probably won't learn about myself or sharpen my skills
☐	☐	☐

Comments: _____

_____

> If most ticks are in the first column, this indicates that you feel confident you will benefit from direct interaction. You should consider *personal* involvement. If most ticks are in the third column, this suggests that you won't benefit from personal involvement. You should consider taking an *impersonal* stance. For all other tick configurations, *moderate* interaction is likely to be appropriate.
>
> Your interaction: ☐ Personal ☐ Moderate ☐ Impersonal

Choose your strategic style or styles

Now that you have a sense of the degree of flexibility and personal involvement you feel is appropriate to a situation and stakeholder personalities, consult Figure 2 (page 41) and select your strategic style. For example, if you've decided on a *firm* stance and *personal* involvement, note that Figure 2 indicates *domination* as the appropriate strategic style.

A single style may not serve your needs as well as a blend. Suppose Figure 2 indicates *domination,* but your knowledge of the situation and stakeholders suggests a 'softer' approach. You may want to blend *domination* with *smoothing.* In other words, the model serves only two functions:

1. it helps to remind you of the full range of possibilities;
2. it helps you to target an appropriate strategic style.

Override the model if your intuition signals an alternative approach. Even if it should prove to be non-productive, you can generally switch to a back-up or contingency plan later.

PHASE 3
Preparation

Armed with knowledge of how to select appropriate strategic styles, two important steps remain prior to implementation:

1. applying your strategy within a problem-solving framework;
2. practising, with a little help from your friends.

Step 1. Use a problem-solving framework

Applying the diagnostic and strategic steps discussed thus far is, in essence, structured *problem-solving*. Despite the compelling logic of following these steps, in the heat of an argument a problem-solving context is easy to forget. Consider the following situation.

Case study 2: The start-up*

George: I don't believe my ears! You waited until now to tell me you're enrolling in college for the coming year to work on your degree? You haven't been inside a classroom in five years. You know I'm struggling to get my business off the ground, and we need your income.

Monica: I've told you before – I'm bored stiff with my job. I want more challenge and a chance to grow. It's about time I did something for me.

---

* This case was adapted from J H Frost and W W Wilmot, *Interpersonal Conflict*, Wm C Brown Company, 1978.

George: I'm working 12 hours a day, and you want to be Mrs Graduate. I thought you understood me when I said I need to buy new equipment to be competitive. Look, Monica, if you wait just two more years, I'll have a going operation with enough money so you can enrol in the best college around.

Monica: How do I know we'll be any better off two years from now?

Continue the dialogue below. If you're a man, assume you are Monica's husband; if you're a woman, continue the dialogue as though you are George's wife. In either case, provide dialogue for both George and Monica consistent with your strategic style.

George: _____

_____

_____

Monica: _____

_____

_____

George: _____

_____

_____

Monica: _____

_____

_____

When workshop participants are asked to continue this dialogue, they generally opt for a *bargaining* strategy in which both parties seek a compromise solution.

Women taking Monica's role (most popular responses):
- Going to college is important to me, but I'd be willing to go part-time or during the evening.
- Maybe I can get a grant to ease the financial burden.
- I'd be willing to continue working full-time and going to college during the evening if you would help more around the house.

Men taking George's role (most popular responses):
- It's important to get this business off to a good start. It has the potential to be a big money-maker. Then you can give up your job and do whatever you like.
- I'm happy for you to get a grant or go to college in the evenings. I'm willing to help around the house.
- Why don't you try working part-time and going to college part-time? If it doesn't work out, at least it will give us time to work out what else we can do.

Because these comments are made without the benefit of a diagnostic and strategic framework, participants usually miss some vital considerations. The problem-solving framework presented earlier in this book is useful.

1. Clarify critical issues
2. Identify stakeholders
3. Assess likely sources of conflict
4. Recognise patterns and minimise blocks
5. Plan your strategy.

Reference to this framework offers ideas you might otherwise miss. For example, in the Monica-George situation, the outline opens additional constructive possibilities.

1. Clarify critical issues
What's awry between Monica and George is the gap between what is versus what's wanted. What's explicitly wanted and

missing is *adequate financing for the business* if Monica simultaneously prepares for a more *interesting career*. What's *implicitly* wanted, and seems from the dialogue to be missing, is respectful communication that can support a *satisfying marital relationship*.

2. Identify stakeholders

Stakeholders Monica and George have an equal claim to realising their separate and joint objectives. Yet George assumes a patriarchal role. He acts as though he has a greater stake in the outcome of the disagreement and, therefore, greater power. He says, 'I'm struggling to get *my* business off the ground ... so that *I* can enrol you in the best college around.' Interestingly, when men and women extend the dialogue, both sexes typically have Monica making the concessions to win George's approval. Even when they let George concede to helping around the house, Monica still keeps most of the responsibility.

3. Assess likely sources of conflict

- The business needs more capital than it can now generate.

  Possibilities. Apply for a grant. Seek outside funding. Reduce cash needs by leasing rather than buying new equipment. Reduce expenses by replacing an employee with Monica who would work at least part-time in the business.

- Monica wants a more exciting job and she wants to develop her career potential.

  Possibilities. Make George's business the *family's* business with Monica a full partner. Take courses that would help Monica to contribute to the success of the business. Apply for a student grant. Go on a sandwich course.

4. Recognise patterns and minimise blocks

Their dialogue suggests that Monica and George have a competitive pattern. Instead of exploring and supporting each other's needs, both husband and wife use dysfunctional personal styles.

Monica withholds information until it's too late for George to upset her plan for returning to study. George demeans Monica (violating guiding principle 1: 'Preserve dignity') using 'Mrs Graduate' as a deflating barb. A barrier keeping the couple from experiencing a more loving relationship may be their defensiveness. Monica protects herself from what she perceives as George's superior power; George may feel threatened by the prospect of Monica's personal growth or financial independence.

5. *Plan your strategy*
The polarised positions (George's business versus Monica's study) that the couple have taken, leave room only for a competitive strategy, such as *bargaining*. Bargaining is appropriate for a labour management dispute, or wherever a win-win solution isn't feasible. Bargaining rarely fosters closeness, however, in an intimate relationship. In contrast, *collaboration* enables the partners to confront the disagreement directly by fully disclosing their needs and concerns. Through collaboration, George and Monica can diagnose the real problems, deal with blocks, and resolve the issues creatively and with goodwill.

As you re-read the dialogue you wrote for George and Monica, did you use a problem-solving framework? Most people don't. Constructive conflict resolution takes lots of practice, especially in emotional situations. If you had incorporated the five-step framework just reviewed, would your strategic approach have been richer?

Here is another opportunity to practise problem-solving. Consider the following case involving people in an organisation.

Case study 3: Serving the customer
Pat is marketing manager for Transitex, a company that manufactures electronic products. After receiving two complaints, Pat phoned a random sample of recent customers and discovered that the problem was not an isolated case. Several orders were despatched late, or errors were made in what was sent. Some irate customers had already given their business to competitors.

Pat decided that this situation must be dealt with now, and prevented from recurring in the future. With support from top management, Pat created a new position – customer coordinator – to periodically check customer satisfaction, decide whether procedures needed to be changed and initiate corrective action.

The general attitude of most employees to Pat's announcement was: 'This, too, will pass.' The company frequently created improvement programmes that proved ineffectual and later were dropped or withered away. Sensing that employees were at odds with the customer-coordinator plan, Pat deferred interviewing candidates for the new position until the disagreement was constructively resolved.

If you were Pat, how would you handle this disagreement between management and the workers? Use the space below to write your action plan.

_____

_____

_____

_____

_____

_____

_____

_____

_____

The most common responses to the situation are: shape up the despatch department; ask workers for their ideas on why despatches are going out late or are inaccurate; and provide incentives for workers to improve their performance.

While these are reasonable suggestions, a problem-solving

framework enables your diagnosis to be richer and your strategic plan more focused.

1. *Clarify critical issues.* Customers are dissatisfied, business is being lost and employees are disgruntled.
2. *Identify stakeholders.* In addition to marketing and warehouse personnel, others who may be involved in the problem include managers and workers in manufacturing, quality control, stock control and personnel training. Executive management, shareholders and major customers also have a stake in the issues.
3. *Assess likely sources of conflict.* When a problem develops in a sequential process, it's often useful to follow the flow. In this case, the process starts when a sale is made.

Concerns that are *sales related* and deserve examination are:
- Have sales personnel quoted realistic delivery dates?
- Is there an adequate system for special handling of high-priority orders?
- Can sales demand be predicted more accurately so that adequate stock levels will not create shipping delays?

Because orders are filled from *stock*, additional questions to consider include:
- Does Transitex have an adequate stock control system?
- Are purchased components being delivered on schedule?
- Are quality control standards being satisfied?

With respect to *despatch*, these questions are pertinent:
- Are warehouse personnel being selected, trained and motivated appropriately?
- Are proper forwarders (road, rail, parcels service, postal service) being used?

Information also needs to be gathered on these *general* questions:
- What follow-up should be provided, to ensure customer satisfaction?
- What organisational, production or shipping changes, if any,

were recently made that may be related to the current problems?

- What, if anything, is the competition doing differently?

4. *Recognise patterns and minimise blocks.* Management seems to be following a pattern, particularly with regard to previous 'improvement' programmes (and violating guiding principle 2: 'Listen with empathy'). Managers should explore how well they listen, and how flexibly they respond to compelling alternative views.

5. *Plan your strategy.* Managers were so aloof and authoritarian in the past that workers now feel apathetic and resentful. More personal involvement, coupled with open-minded flexibility, is indicated. The resultant *collaborative* strategic style is likely to produce constructive results if stakeholder representatives are brought into the picture with enough orientation, so they will want to become involved in the process. (*Note.* When you plan to use any style, introduce it in a manner appropriate to the style. For example, introduce collaboration through discussion, not by a memo directing: 'This group will collaborate!')

Step 2. Practise

You have now reviewed working with disagreements in a problem-solving context. For contrast, you were given an emotionally charged *personal* disagreement and a technically oriented *organisational* disagreement. Both provided practice with a *collaborative* style.

Exercise 5 is designed to help you practise a *full range* of strategic styles. The idea is to build confidence in a low-risk setting through *role playing* those styles you currently under-use.

This is where you can use help from your friends, because *two other people* are needed. After you've enlisted two friends or colleagues, teach them each of the nine styles for managing disagreement. (Exercise 5 will also help you to remember the full range of available strategies.)

Start each role-play by announcing the style you intend to

practise first. Note that in dealing with real disagreements, you will often blend styles. However, at this point, practise with a *single style* in each role-play situation to gain mastery.

One approach is to invent, recall or rehearse something that actually happened, or you may prefer to use the workshop-tested situations presented in subsequent pages. Note that the description of each role-play situation is purposely sketchy so you can add information pertinent to actual circumstances in your work and personal life. Pick a situation that feels natural so you have no need to act. Just be yourself using a new style.

Before starting your role-play, review it with your colleagues to be sure that everyone understands the background facts you are adding, and any revisions you may want to incorporate in the situation.

Have one person play the 'other party' or 'foil' who will provide the differing point of view. The 'foil' should not too quickly abandon his or her position, but should keep the dispute going for as long as would be realistic under the circumstances. On the other hand, when the 'skill-builder' moves fully into the desired strategic style, the 'foil' should respond constructively.

Ask your other friend to take the role of the 'observer'. The 'observer' is to witness without comment, and is encouraged to take brief notes based on the 'Observer guide', which starts on page 69.

The 'Observer guide' is a valuable resource, worth careful review. It describes *observable behaviour* associated with each of the nine strategic styles when they are skilfully used.

Following each role-play, allow a few minutes for personal note-taking and time for everyone to provide feedback observations and reactions. Pay particular attention to whether or not you (the 'skill-builder') slipped out of the style you intended to practise and into a style that feels more familiar to you.

Before moving on to a second 'style', ask your friends if they want a turn. If so, simply rotate roles until each person has held all three positions: the skill-builder, the foil and the observer.

Exercise 5: Style trial situations

Style 1 • Maintenance

1. You just received very upsetting news from home that deserves your immediate personal attention. A moment later, your secretary tells you that a major client has arrived for an appointment you set up to discuss a sensitive issue on which only you can provide the needed help. Something must be said to this client.

2. A new customer phones your secretary and threatens to sue your organisation for an injury that occurred while the customer was allegedly using a product your company manufactures. You made the sale. Your secretary transfers the call to your office, and you pick up the phone.

Style 2 • Smoothing

3. Recently, you started receiving personal phone calls during working hours. While you've enjoyed these calls, you realise they are interfering with your work. You decide they may hurt your career if they continue. When you receive your next personal call, you say: '. . .'

4. A customer phones and *insists* that you personally handle the specific details of a purchase, as you have in the past. However, since your last contact with this customer – whose business is valued, but not of major consequence – you have been promoted. Your secretary tried to explain that your new position has taken you out of the customer-relations area, but without success. Now it's up to you to speak to this customer.

Style 3 • Domination

5. Your car was repaired and you were assured by the garage mechanic that the problem was remedied. When you took a test drive round the block, it seemed all right, and you paid your bill. Three days later, the old symptoms recurred indicating that the problem was not correctly diagnosed. You have now returned to the garage and want your car to be

repaired promptly and properly. You don't intend to make any additional payment.

6. Your managing director was appointed to the executive board of United Way, a community charity. She is eager to have all employees contribute. Probably because of the MD's full employee participation target, the company fund committee has been zealous to the point of becoming obnoxious. The committee sent you three memos despite your polite but firm 'not this year' replies. The fund committee chairman just walked into your office unannounced to persuade you personally to make a donation. You intend to tell him to stop badgering you.

Style 4 ● Decision rule

7. You plan to buy a car soon. To date, you've collected information on prices, safety, petrol consumption, features, reliability, road handling performance, resale value and running costs. Styling is also very important to you. Your family is getting impatient with your data gathering activities, and everyone wants to have some say in the final decision. You would be happy with any one of three cars. (Role play with one 'family member'.)

8. At work, a rush project has come up that needs two people to work overtime this coming weekend. Of the people reporting to you, five say that they want to work on the project because they would like the extra pay. All five are equally capable of handling the job without supervision. You have to choose two of these volunteers because the work can't be divided among all five. (Role play with one 'representative' employee.)

Style 5 ● Coexistence

9. Mothers-in-law are often portrayed as difficult, overbearing people. Your relationship with your mother-in-law fits this stereotypical image perfectly. If you say 'black', she says 'white'. In fact, you see eye-to-eye on virtually nothing. She is visiting for the weekend and has just lectured you on how to bring up your children. Despite your obvious discomfort

with her views, she spared no detail on what you are doing wrong and the dire consequences to your children's future development. You respond to her monologue by saying: '...'

10. Your department is using a manual system for stock control which has worked extremely well over many years. Your recently completed analysis, however, convinces you that the system should be automated. You predict added flexibility and, after a breaking-in period, substantial savings. Carmen is also a departmental manager and her unit operates in parallel with your group. She disagrees with your analysis. Her concerns are employee resistance, a system that is more vulnerable to error and the disruption created whenever the system is down. You've arranged to meet Carmen to discuss your differences. At the meeting, you start the conversation.

Style 6 ● Bargaining

11. You've just moved to a new city to accept a position that represents an important career opportunity. Unfortunately, as you arrived, your car broke down beyond repair. Your job, which starts in two days, demands a car. A newspaper advertisement offers a used car well suited to your needs and your tight budget. A phone call and a taxi ride takes you to the car you want, but the asking price is more than you can afford. To complicate matters, you haven't yet established credit locally and have only a modest down payment with you. You optimistically decide to negotiate the purchase of this car.

    (In 'bargaining' scenarios, the person acting as the foil can add realism by privately developing specific bargaining goals. In this case, for example, a minimum selling price and terms of sale should be set – and told only to the observer – before the action starts.)

12. You've been assigned to a company task force with an exciting mission and opportunity for top management visibility. The assignment means moving to a new office to be shared with another task force member. After the move, you discover that your office-mate is a smoker. You strongly

object to smoke in your working space, and your company has no policy that covers this problem. You decide to speak to your new office-mate about it.

Style 7 • Non-resistance

13. You agreed to support the position a colleague told you she was presenting at an important strategy meeting. During the meeting, after your friend made her presentation, a key executive forcefully criticised her plan. Instead of rallying to her defence as you had promised, and bringing up points you could endorse, you remained silent. Now, later in the day, your colleague enters your office and tells you how terribly disappointed she is with your lack of support at the meeting. You reply, saying: '...'

14. Your boss has been full of new ideas lately. Sadly, from your point of view, he intended to implement two that were not only off-target, but would have delayed your current project, added expense and reduced quality. On both occasions you had to explain to your boss why his ideas would hamper progress. Now he's come up with a third idea that you again feel is not helpful. However, not much is at stake, no adverse precedents would be set, and the downside consequences are minor. When asked for your views, you say: '...'

Style 8 • Supportive release

15. Your daughter, Suzanne, received her degree three years ago, landed a good-paying job and has been able to build up her savings by living rent-free at home. You feel the time has come for your daughter to leave the nest and get her own flat. When you talk to Suzanne, you learn that she feels really comfortable at home and isn't thinking of leaving.

16. Barbara will take over your department when your announced promotion takes effect next week. She's done an outstanding job and you've been grooming her to assume added responsibilities. Today, she asked to meet you to propose a departmental reorganisation. While you want her to take more initiative, you disagree with Barbara's proposal, and feel it won't provide the benefits she anticipates. On the

other hand, even if it isn't an improvement, the plan can't do much harm. You say to Barbara: '...'

Style 9 • Collaboration

17. You recently got married and, after three blissful months, are facing some cold realities. The problems in your otherwise happy relationship cluster around 'practicality'. Your partner has overdrawn your joint bank account twice in the past month. You decide to discuss your bank account in particular, and household budgeting in general.

18. Your boss, Tom, calls you into his office to discuss a project report you've been asked to submit to the board. Tom tells you it's in order to exaggerate progress during the last quarter. He says that this 'white lie' will avoid needless embarrassing questions. Tom assures you that, although the project has lagged behind schedule, those delays soon will be made up. You are uncomfortable with the ethical implication of your boss's request.

Observer guide

While observing a role-player managing disagreement, note the behaviour patterns in the space provided (see pages 70–71). Particularly, look for the listed behaviour styles because they support the strategic style that the role-player is attempting to advance.

Strategic style/Observable behaviour	Observer's Notes
● *Maintenance*	
Use delaying tactics.	
Remain non-reactive and calm.	
Don't make commitments; don't make concessions.	
● *Smoothing*	
Provide information selectively.	
Accentuate areas of agreement.	
Minimise the importance of differences.	
● *Domination*	
Make your position crystal clear.	
Express conviction; don't equivocate.	
Describe the consequence of non-compliance.	
● *Decision rule*	
Get agreement on the options to be decided.	
Get agreement on an objective rule to be used.	
Get agreement to support whatever the outcome.	
● *Coexistence*	
Define the separate courses of action.	
Decide how long to follow divergent paths.	
Get agreement on how to evaluate results.	

Strategic style/Observable behaviour	Observer's notes
• *Bargaining*	
Clarify interests of both parties.	
Define the 'zone of mutual benefit' – where both parties gain.	
Develop options for mutual benefit.	
Make offers and evaluate counter-offers.	
• *Non-resistance*	
Clarify expectations and state reservations.	
Offer full support if reservations are accepted.	
Decide on alternatives if the proposed action fails.	
• *Supportive release*	
Clarify expectations and state reservations.	
Empower the other person adequately.	
Describe the nature and limits of your support.	
• *Collaboration*	
Disclose your interests and concerns.	
Listen without defending your position.	
Avoid converging too quickly on one alternative.	
Problem-solve to develop alternatives that satisfy all interests and concerns.	

PHASE 4
Implementation

Your final phase in managing disagreement constructively deserves the same care as those which led up to this point.

Step 1. Carry out the plan

Several considerations in implementing your plan require close attention. These are:

- A productive emotional atmosphere
- Compatible strategies and breaking deadlocks
- Building implementive skills
- Blending strategic styles and closing constructively.

The emotional side of disagreement

When people disagree and voice their views, an informed decision can be made. However, many people are reluctant to express disagreement openly in a variety of situations. They are concerned about hurting feelings, damaging relationships and dealing with out-of-control emotional reactions.

The challenge in handling feelings is to allow them to be talked about openly. A line needs to be drawn between table-thumping rage that intimidates and simply saying you are angry. Strong feelings can be used to bully, while unexpressed and unresolved feelings can bias good judgement. For example, people reject good ideas because they are angry with the individuals expressing them.

The more common concern, both in organisational and

personal relationships, is *unexpressed emotion*. To the extent that you risk disclosing *your* feelings as you deal with differences, others will feel safer expressing what they are experiencing. You can communicate your feelings directly, saying: 'I feel frustrated,' 'I feel embarrassed'; or by using similes, such as: 'I feel stepped on,' 'I don't feel heard.'

The expression of feelings while managing disagreement serves to:

- Provide *problem-solving feedback*. Negative feelings signal that something valued is amiss.
- Make *relevant input discussable*. By avoiding a potentially emotional topic, information is lost that could lead to creative solutions.
- *Connect people more personally*. When we get to know one another as people with feelings, rather than merely as proponents of viewpoints, chances for working together constructively are vastly improved. When we communicate our 'humanness', we take a giant step towards reaching common ground.

In summary, our feelings enable others to clarify misperceptions and to join us in real, rather than role, relationships.

Compatible strategies and breaking deadlocks
If stakeholders choose strategies that don't fit together compatibly, disagreement ends in a deadlock or a fragile truce.

Strategies that lead to deadlocks
Deadlocks occur when two parties remain unyielding in their positions or keep sparring for control. Such stalemates are predictable when dominance or smoothing strategies are pitted against one another.

- **Domination** is functional only when one person has the *power and resources* to direct another, the *understanding* to appreciate the situation and its implications, and a *willing follower*. In the absence of any of these conditions, dominance usually leads to the use of counter-dominance. When power is about equal, a stalemate results. When power isn't equal and the disagreement is pushed underground, it ultimately surfaces as resistance or erupts into full-blown conflict.

- **Smoothing** is an effective strategy when one party to the disagreement is *receptive*. On the other hand, two 'smoothers' will slide into an impasse because both are selling and no one is buying. Either the arguments aren't persuasive, aren't relevant, or the people simply aren't listening to one another. A sale can't be made to those who are preoccupied with fine-tuning their own sales pitch.

The remaining incompatibility is collaboration opposed by *any* of the three 'firm' strategies (domination, smoothing and maintenance) because collaborators must be willing to consider alternative views. This is quickly seen in Figure 2 (page 41).

Breaking deadlocks

To break a deadlock caused by any strategic mismatch, use one of the three 'moderately firm' styles (bargaining, coexistence and decision rule).

- **Bargaining** allows people, whose horns are locked in domination and counter-domination, to back off. Note that while tough battlers resist being seen as 'soft', they can still fight the 'good fight' within a bargaining framework.

- **Coexistence** breaks an impasse when two clear options are available. In such cases, one party can pursue one course of action, while the other takes a different approach on an experimental basis. In advance of such an experiment, stakeholders must agree on criteria for assessing the outcomes, and when to end the experiment.

- **Decision rule,** the quickest way to break a deadlock, requires workable options to be identified and agreeing to a *fair and clear procedure* for selecting one. This may be a lottery, vote, seniority system, arbitration or any objective criterion. For example, when boys fight over who gets which piece of cake, the dispute can be settled using as the *clear and fair procedure*: one cuts the cake, the other gets first choice.

Building implementive skills

Of the nine strategic styles for managing disagreement, *two* require special attention. To *collaborate* or *bargain* successfully, you need to have interpersonal skills in conformity with the character of each process. The following guidelines will help you to apply these styles skilfully.

- **Collaboration,** also called consensual decision-making. This is a win-win strategy based on self-disclosure and mutual *trust*. All cards must be put face up on the table. Participant differences are resolved when they reach an agreement that reasonably satisfies all expressed needs and aspirations. The following steps lead to constructive collaboration.

  1. *Don't impose a solution.* The basic ground rule is that a collective view must emerge neither from coercion nor majority vote, but from forthright, empathetic discussion.
  2. *Provide background information.* Stakeholders must present their views with enough background for others to see them in context. Say what really matters to you, including your assumptions, hopes and fears.
  3. *Don't surrender your view to reduce group tension.* If you throw in the towel to be a 'Mr Nice' or to avoid the heat of confrontation, you deny others the benefit of your insights and reasoning. You probably won't feel committed to whatever is decided. (Note this application of guiding principle 4: 'Express your independent perspective'.)
  4. *Actively invite different views.* This is not a win-lose competition. Everyone can win, but only when the richness of diverse views is honestly expressed and then creatively blended.
  5. *Search deeply for understanding.* Listen to others respectfully to appreciate their insights. Honour their disclosures as you would a valued gift. Allow some time for silent reflection. Test your understanding with the speaker on complex issues.
  6. *Keep testing ideas for group acceptance.* As you integrate ideas, keep checking to determine when relevant interests are satisfied and concerns adequately addressed.

- **Bargaining** is a *mixed-motive* strategy. You walk a tightrope between cooperation and competition, seeking a compromise agreement to reconcile differences. For example, lawyers trying to settle a dispute out of court can save their clients court expense by cooperating with one another. However, to win the best deal, they need to compete. Therefore, bargaining requires, not the candid disclosure of collaboration, but *guarded manoeuvring* between 'cooperative antagonists'. Benjamin Franklin captured the essence of bargaining:

  > 'Trades would not take place unless it were advantageous to the parties concerned. Of course, it is better to strike as good a bargain as one's bargaining position permits. The worst outcome is when, by overreaching greed, no bargain is struck, and a trade that would have been advantageous to both parties does not come off at all.'

Generally, you will want to deal with people who are sincere, use their power with grace and can be counted on to honour agreements. The following guidelines offer specific suggestions for bargaining constructively:

1. *Have precise objectives and support for them.* When you know what you want and have a thoughtful rationale, your position gains *legitimacy*. If you're selling a home, for example, support your asking price with recent sales data on comparable houses in the neighbourhood.
2. *Check that a mutually beneficial agreement is possible.* Probe early to discover if a *zone of mutual benefit* exists without giving away your specific intentions. For buyer-seller situations, this zone would be the *price range where both would benefit*. But, within this zone, buyers jockey for a low-end price, while sellers manoeuvre to close the deal towards the upper end.
3. *Consider a third-party mediator.* If parties are reluctant to share information directly, they may be willing to use an impartial, ethical intermediary. A third party can often assure disputants that a zone of mutual benefit actually exists. Mediators also can help by: letting highly charged emotions vent; recasting issues in more acceptable terms; facilitating communication;

and developing ground rules, such as holding the meeting at a neutral venue, and setting time limits.

4. *To strike a favourable bargain, consider the following tactics.*

- *Give concessions grudgingly.* After you present objective standards to support your position, make only small concessions and do so reluctantly. Generous, quickly made concessions undermine your credibility.
- *Give concessions in exchange for concessions.* Offer your concessions as 'I will ... if you will ...' When you ask for reciprocity, your non-verbal statement is, 'I want to help us keep moving towards agreement, but I don't intend to give away the shop in the process.'
- *Separate the issues.* You may soften resistance on critical issues if you offer concessions on issues that have only minor consequence for you. This tactic may also help the other person to save face by not appearing to yield to all your demands.
- *Relate your bargaining stance to the other person's needs.* Instead of saying, 'I need a higher salary,' keep your boss's needs in mind. Say, for example, 'Let me show you what I've done and will continue to do to improve the company's bottom line.' Instead of, 'I want a more generous divorce settlement,' a more compelling position is, 'More money is needed to send the kids to a better school.'
- *Limit your authority.* Paradoxically, in bargaining, less authority is more power. Salespeople who can't grant discounts, and buyers who can't exceed budgets, don't make concessions in those areas. Also, if you have to defer to a higher authority, you gain time to think through a difficult concern.

Blending strategic styles

For clarity, each style has been described as though it is implemented in its pure form. In reality, styles are often combined to create a hybrid or blend. The two most common blends are elaborated below.

Blend 1

- *Domination-smoothing*. This blend is effective when you want to be forceful in your conviction and persuasive in your presentation. An appropriate application is the supervision of an employee who violates an important company policy. The supervisor wants to be certain the policy is followed, and also wants the employee to be convinced the policy is sound so she won't violate it covertly.

Blend 2

- *Bargaining-collaboration*. This is such a common blend that it has its own name – *negotiation*.* Situations appropriate for this blend occur when you can help yourself by also helping the other party. If, when you start *slicing* what appears to be a fixed 'pie' through bargaining, you see an opportunity for *enlarging* the pie, start collaborating. This can be done by exploring common interests. For example, suppose you are bargaining over how to divide a crate of oranges. Within this bargaining framework, you can invite collaboration by disclosing: 'I'm interested in oranges because I want the rind for baking. Why are *you* interested in them?' If the other person's answer is 'Juice!' you've uncovered a juicy win-win solution.

Closing constructively

Just as sales people focus attention on closing a sale, you need to concern yourself with the *final steps* in translating your differences into agreement. Here are some helpful guidelines.

1. *Document your agreement*. Even personal agreements between parents and children are more effective when written down. A carefully typed statement demonstrates commitment, and provides a reference for the future when memories get hazy.

---

* Excellent books on negotiating are: *Successful Negotiation* by Robert Maddux and *Never Take No For an Answer* by Samfrits Le Poole, both published by Kogan Page.

2. *Draft your agreement as discussions progress.* As you search for words to phrase your agreement, the intentions of both parties will be clarified. Participants will also see what issues, terms and conditions remain on the agenda to be resolved.

3. *Decide how results will be monitored.* What will be measured? How? By whom? For how long? What will constitute a successful outcome? Get commitments from individuals to deadlines for completing specific responsibilities.

4. *Discuss what happens if . . .* A big 'if' to consider is the possibility of non-performance. Whether a legally binding contract, or a note taped on the refrigerator door to distribute household chores, the *consequences* of not living up to the agreement should be agreed in advance.

5. *Help the other person to sell the agreement 'back home'.* Find out if your disputant needs further approval or ratification. If so, strengthen his or her hand by rehearsing arguments helpful in persuading others to go along.

6. *Set a realistic deadline.* Is timely closure important to you? If so, indicate why. Perhaps if you don't resolve your differences by next Tuesday, you can't guarantee delivery, or hold the interest rate, or ensure approval. Deadlines stir action.

Step 2. Evaluate outcomes

The purpose of evaluation is twofold:

1. to initiate any *corrective or adaptive action* that may be needed as the situation unfolds and hazy assumptions are clarified; and

2. to *learn* from your experience so that future disagreements will be handled better.

Evaluate the need for corrective or adaptive action

To evaluate the outcome of a disagreement, weigh your results against a comprehensive set of *criteria*. The five presented here are useful for this purpose. To demonstrate how to apply these criteria to a specific disagreement, let's return to the 'Petty cash' case on page 17 where Edwin and Henry initially had divergent views about how to handle Mary's breach of trust.

- *Technical.* Is the resolution you've come up with *technically feasible?*

Example: In the 'Petty cash' case, replacing cash advances to travellers with plastic cards for automated-teller machines is workable, and even more convenient because the machines are accessible 24 hours a day.

- *Economic.* Is the solution more *efficient* than the old system?

Example: The use of credit cards versus cash advances will save money because accounting is handled by the bank and auditing is less costly.

- *Social-psychological.* Will resolution of differences maintain social harmony without adverse *interpersonal or emotional* side effects?

Example: If Mary is retained, a method of disciplining her would need to be found that didn't start the grapevine buzzing with rumours about her performance.

- *Ethical-legal.* Would implementing your solution be *legal, moral and fair*?

Example: Henry's concern in this case turned on the issue of fairness. He didn't believe it was fair to fire one employee tempted by a lax system and under emotional duress, while other employees were 'stealing' from the company in the form of lost productivity by their marginal efforts, lateness and long lunches. Accordingly, Henry's recommendation to Edwin was to put Mary on a two-year probation, confidentially document the affair and arrange for systematic repayment.

- *Political.* Will your agreement be supported by those in positions of *power*?

Example: In the 'Petty cash' case (a true story), Henry was so concerned about the 'Mary incident' that he discussed it fully with his board of directors. Before action was taken, he had their support.

Personal learning

By taking time to reflect on how you manage disagreements, you will keep improving your performance. A helpful approach to self-examination is to review each of the four phases of managing disagreements: diagnosis, planning, preparation and implementation. (For your convenience they are summarised on pages 83 to 85.) The following questions will help to guide your introspection.

- *Diagnosis*
  - Did you collect enough information, or were you impatient? Were the people from whom you got information reliable, or were you naive?
  - Did you accurately pinpoint the information, goals, methods and feelings that were at the heart of the disagreement?

- *Planning*
  - Did you consider a full range of strategic styles, and choose an appropriate one or an appropriate blend? If not, did you opt for a familiar strategy with which you are more comfortable?

- *Preparation*
  - Did you anticipate the key issues? If not, were you underprepared?
  - Did too much rehearsal hinder you from responding creatively to the unexpected?

- *Implementation*
  - Were you able, in your intervention, to build an appropriate level of mutual trust and respect? If not, what got in the way?
  - Did you marshal adequate resources and enlist the support you needed? If not, did you operate too independently?

Step 3. Take follow-up action

Your evaluation will suggest whether any follow-up activity is needed. Clearly, if the outcome is off target, remedial action is appropriate. Even if a dispute is reconciled constructively, some monitoring and reinforcement helps to ensure that commitments will be kept.

To catch disagreement before it escalates into conflict, you may want to design formal systems for airing grievances. In families, this can be as simple as a weekly round table where parents and children can discuss anything that feels awry. Organisational justice systems include supervisory training in managing disagreement, a grievance appeals process and use of an ombudsman. Empowered to speak with everyone including top executives, the ombudsman cannot mandate action but helps to clear up misunderstandings.

For your personal growth, take time to *record* the key points in your management of important disagreements. From these notes you will more clearly see where future improvements can be made. Identify the skills you want to develop further, and follow up on them.

Reflection

Dealing constructively with disagreement has profound impact. We open ourselves to making real contact with others. We complete unfinished business. Our vision of what's possible expands.

Every human being is unique. Disagreement reflects that uniqueness. When we are able to do something constructive with our differences, we move closer to the ideal of one human family living together in a peaceful, productive and satisfying world.

Summary

The following is your roadmap to managing disagreement constructively. Refer to it often.

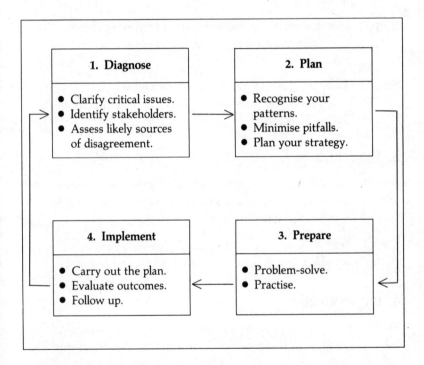

1. Diagnosis

Step 1. *Clarify critical issues.* After you've developed your *initial* position, find out whether others agree with your views. If not, identify areas of difference on key issues.

Step 2. *Identify stakeholders*, those persons who have a vested interest in the outcome of the disagreement. (Often taken concurrently with Step 1.)

Step 3. *Assess likely sources* of potential conflict: information, goals, methods or antagonistic feelings.

2. Planning

Step 1. *Recognise your patterns*, those characteristic styles you've developed over the years for handling disagreement.

Step 2. *Minimise pitfalls* to choosing an appropriate strategy. Guard against being rigid, irresolute, intrusive or aloof.

Step 3. *Plan your strategy* to advance common goals, gain acceptance by other stakeholders, permit timely action and efficient use of resources.

3. Preparation

Step 1. *Problem-solve* using the preceding steps as a framework to refine your diagnosis and more sharply focus your strategic plan.

Step 2. *Practise.* Rehearse strategies unfamiliar to you with friends from whom you can gain candid feedback.

4. Implementation

Step 1. *Carry out your plan* paying attention to the physical setting and emotional atmosphere, skill level and style compatibility of the disputants, time constraints and need for documentation.

Step 2. *Evaluate outcomes* to reinforce the agreement, adapt to new circumstances, or take corrective action. Use technical, economic, social-psychological, ethical-legal and political evaluation criteria.

Step 3. *Take follow-up action* as indicated by your evaluation. Consider future monitoring, particularly if unforeseen factors have emerged.

Nine strategic styles for managing differences

	Style 3 **DOMINATION** You unilaterally induce, persuade, force compliance or resist.	Style 6 **BARGAINING** You jointly seek means to split differences, set trade-offs or take turns.	Style 9 **COLLABORATION** You jointly problem-solve to integrate views.
highly personal			
moderately personal	Style 2 **SMOOTHING** You unilaterally accentuate similarities and play down differences.	Style 5 **COEXISTENCE** You jointly establish a basis for both parties to maintain their differences.	Style 8 **SUPPORTIVE RELEASE** You unilaterally release the issue, stipulate any limits and provide needed support.
impersonal	Style 1 **MAINTENANCE** You unilaterally avoid confronting differences or delay making changes.	Style 4 **DECISION RULE** You jointly set objective rules that determine how differences will be handled.	Style 7 **NON-RESISTANCE** You offer no resistance to the other party's views, blending your efforts with theirs.

INTENSITY OF INTERACTION

FLEXIBILITY OF VIEWPOINT

firm	moderately flexible	flexible

Further Reading

This book offers concise, practical coverage of managing disagreement. The following books are more theoretical. Following each reference, the book's general orientation is indicated.

Morton Deutsch, *The Resolution of Conflict: Constructive and Destructive Processes*, Yale University Press, 1973. This is a highly readable book comprised of theoretical essays and research papers ranging from intrapsychic to international conflict.

Howard Raiffa, *The Art and Science of Negotiation*, Harvard University Press, 1982. Provides a systematic analysis for the problem-solving of disputes including ethical and moral issues.

Roger Fisher and William Ury, *Getting To Yes*, Hutchinson, 1983. Concise, coherent book on principled negotiation including practical bargaining tactics.

Further reading from Kogan Page

How to Develop Assertiveness: Practical Techniques for Personal Success,
   Sam R Lloyd
Never Take No For an Answer, Samfrits Le Poole
Study Skills Strategies: How to Learn More in Less Time,
   Uelaine Lengefeld
Successful Self-Management: A Sound Approach to Personal Effectiveness,
   Paul R Timm

Better Management Skills

Effective Meeting Skills: How to Make Meetings More Productive,
  Marion E Haynes
Effective Performance Appraisals, Robert B Maddux
Effective Presentation Skills, Steve Mandel
The Fifty-Minute Supervisor: A Guide for the Newly Promoted,
  Elwood N Chapman
How to Develop a Positive Attitude, Elwood N Chapman
Make Every Minute Count: How to Manage Your Time Effectively,
  Marion E Haynes
Successful Negotiation, Robert B Maddux
Team Building: An Exercise in Leadership, Robert B Maddux